...4
..12
20
.26
.32
40
45
.49
..51
55
25
57
65
66
67

Patons
patonsyarns.com
©Patons 2010

nted in Canada
#1-897575-66-6

Joy Stripes Hoodie

EASY

SIZES

To fit chest measurement		
6	25 ins	[63.5 cm]
8	26½ ins	[67.5 cm]
10	28 ins	[71 cm]
12	30 ins	[76 cm]

Finished chest		
6	30 ins	[76 cm]
8	32 ins	[81.5 cm]
10	34 ins	[86.5 cm]
12	36 ins	[91.5 cm]

TENSION

14 sts and 11 rows = 4 ins [10 cm] in pat.

MATERIALS

Patons® Canadiana (100 g/3.5 oz; 187 m /205 yds)						
GIRL'S VERSION	Sizes	6	8	10	12	
	Main Color (MC) 10435 (Coral Rose)	2	2	3	3	balls
	Contrast A 10610 (Fool's Gold)	1	1	2	2	ball(s)
	Contrast B 10744 (Med Teal)	1	1	1	2	ball(s)
	Contrast C 10247 (Cedar Green)	1	1	1	2	ball(s)
	Contrast D 10420 (Cherished Pink)	1	1	1	1	ball
BOY'S VERSION	Sizes	6	8	10	12	
	Main Color (MC) 10012 (Toasty Grey)	3	3	3	4	balls
	Contrast A 10145 (Dk Water Blue)	2	2	2	2	balls
	Contrast B 10610 (Fool's Gold)	2	2	2	2	balls

Size 5 mm (U.S. H or 8) crochet hook **or size needed to obtain tension.**

STITCH GLOSSARY
See page 67 for Helpful Hints.
Alt = Alternate(ing).
Approx = Approximately.
Beg = Beginning.
Ch(s) = Chain(s).
Cont = Continue(ity).
Dc = Double crochet.
Pat = Pattern.
Rem = Remaining.
Rep = Repeat.
RS = Right side.
Sc = Single crochet.
Sl st = Slip stitch.
St(s) = Stitch(es).
WS = Wrong side.
Yoh = Yarn over hook.

INSTRUCTIONS

The instructions are written for smallest size. If changes are necessary for larger sizes the instructions will be written thus ( ). Numbers for each size are shown in the same color throughout the pattern. When only one number is given in black, it applies to all sizes.

Stripe Pat for Girls
With MC, 1 row.
With A, 1 row.
With B, 1 row.
With C, 1 row.
With D, 1 row.
These 5 rows form Stripe Pat for Girls.

Stripe Pat for Boys
With MC, 1 row.
With A, 1 row.
With B, 1 row.
These 3 rows form Stripe Pat for Boys.

Note: To join new color, work to last 2 loops on hook. Draw new color through last 2 loops then proceed in new color.

Do not break yarn at end of row. Carry unused yarn loosely along side of work, twisting long floats with working colors.

BACK
**Ribbing: With MC, ch 10.
1st row: (RS). 1 sc in 2nd ch from hook. 1 sc in each ch to end of ch. Turn. 9 sc.
2nd row: Ch 1. Working in back loops only, 1 sc in each sc to end of row. Turn.
Rep last row until work from beg measures 15 (16-17-18) ins [38 (40.5-43-45.5) ins], ending with a WS row. **Do not** fasten off.

Body: 1st row: (RS). With MC, ch 1. Work 53 (56-60-63) sc along side of ribbing. Join A. Turn.
2nd row: (WS). With A, ch 3 (counts as dc). 1 dc in each sc to end of row. Join B. Turn.
3rd row: With B, ch 1. 1 sc in each dc to end of row. Join C for Girl's Version or join MC for Boy's Version. Turn.
First 3 rows of Stripe Pat are completed. Last 2 rows form Pat.

Keeping cont of appropriate Stripe Pat, cont in pat until work from beg measures approx 11½ (12-14-16) ins [29 (30.5-35.5-40.5) cm], ending with a WS row. Fasten off.

Joy Stripes Hoodie

Shape raglans: 1st row: (RS). Miss first **4** (**4**-**5**-**5**) dc. Join appropriate color with sl st to next dc. Ch 1. 1 sc in same st as last sl st. 1 sc in each dc to last **4** (**4**-**5**-**5**) dc. **Turn.** Leave rem sts unworked.

Cont on rem **45** (**48**-**50**-**53**) sts:

2nd row: Ch 3 (counts as dc). 1 dc in each sc to end of row. Turn.

3rd row: Ch 1. *Draw up a loop in each of next 2 dc. Yoh and draw through all loops on hook – sc2tog made. 1 sc in each dc to last 2 dc. Sc2tog. Turn.***

Rep last 2 rows **3** (**4**-**4**-**6**) times more. **37** (**38**-**40**-**39**) sts.

Next row: (WS). Ch 3 (counts as dc). *(Yoh and draw up a loop in next st. Yoh and draw through 2 loops on hook) twice. Yoh and draw through all loops on hook – dc2tog made.* 1 dc in each sc to last 3 sts. Dc2tog. 1 dc in last st. Turn.

Next row: Ch 1. Sc2tog. 1 sc in each dc to last 2 sts. Sc2tog. Turn.

Rep last 2 rows **2** (**2**-**2**-**1**) time(s) more. **25** (**26**-**28**-**31**) sts.

Next row: (WS). Ch 3 (counts as dc). Dc2tog. 1 dc in each sc to last 3 sts. Dc2tog. 1 dc in last st. **23** (**24**-**26**-**29**) sts rem. Fasten off.

FRONT

Work from ** to ** as given for Back.

Rep last 2 rows **0** (**1**-**1**-**2**) time(s) more. **43** (**44**-**46**-**47**) sts.

Next row: Ch 3 (counts as dc). 1 dc in each sc to end of row. Turn.

Divide for front opening: Next row: (RS). Ch 1. Sc2tog. 1 sc in each of next **25** (**25**-**26**-**27**) dc. **Turn.** Leave rem sts unworked.

Left Front: Cont on last **26** (**26**-**27**-**28**) sts:
Next row: (WS). Ch 3 (counts as dc). 1 dc in each st to end of row. Turn.
Next row: Ch 1. Sc2tog. 1 sc in each dc to end of row. Turn.
Rep last 2 rows **1** (**1**-**1**-**2**) time(s) more. **24** (**24**-**25**-**25**) sts.

Next row: (WS). Ch 3. 1 dc in each sc to last 3 sts. Dc2tog. 1 dc in last st. Turn.
Next row: Ch 1. Sc2tog. 1 sc in each dc to end of row. Turn.
Rep last 2 rows **2** (**2**-**2**-**1**) time(s) more. **18** (**18**-**19**-**21**) sts.
Next row: (WS). Ch 3 (counts as dc). 1 dc in each sc to last 3 sts. Dc2tog. 1 dc in last st. **17** (**17**-**18**-**20**) sts rem. Fasten off.

Right Front: 1st row: (RS). With appropriate color, ch **11** (**10**-**10**-**11**). 1 sc in each rem dc to last 2 dc. Sc2tog. Turn.
2nd row: Ch 3 (counts as dc). 1 dc in each of next **14** (**15**-**16**-**16**) sts. 1 dc in each of next **11** (**10**-**10**-**11**) ch. Turn.
Cont on these **26** (**26**-**27**-**28**) sts:
3rd row: Ch 1. 1 sc in each dc to last 2 sts. Sc2tog. Turn.
4th row: Ch 3 (counts as dc). 1 dc in each st to end of row. Turn.
Rep last 2 rows **1** (**1**-**1**-**2**) time(s) more. **24** (**24**-**25**-**25**) sts.
Next row: Ch 1. 1 sc in each dc to last 2 sts. Sc2tog. Turn.

Next row: Ch 3. Dc2tog. 1 dc in each sc to end of row. Turn.
Rep last 2 rows **2** (**2**-**2**-**1**) time(s) more. **18** (**18**-**19**-**21**) sts.
Next row: (WS). Ch 3. Dc2tog. 1 dc in each sc to end of row. **17** (**17**-**18**-**20**) sts rem. Fasten off.

SLEEVES
Ribbing: With MC, ch 10.
1st row: (RS). 1 sc in 2nd ch from hook. 1 sc in each ch to end of ch. Turn. 9 sc.
2nd row: Ch 1. Working in back loops only, 1 sc in each sc to end of row. Turn.
Rep last row until work from beg measures **7** (**7½**-**8**-**8½**) ins [**18** (**19**-**20.5**-**21.5**) cm], ending with a WS row. **Do not** fasten off.

Body: 1st row: (RS). With MC, ch 1. Work **28** (**30**-**32**-**34**) sc along side of ribbing. Join A. Turn.

Cont in Stripe Pat as given for Back as follows:
2nd row: Ch 3 (counts as dc). 1 dc in each sc to end of row. Turn.
3rd row: Ch 1. 2 sc in first dc. 1 sc in each dc to last dc. 2 sc in last dc. Turn.
Rep last 2 rows **4** (**4**-**4**-**2**) times more. **38** (**40**-**42**-**40**) sts.

Work 3 rows even in pat.
Next row: Ch 1. 2 sc in first dc. 1 sc in each dc to last dc. 2 sc in last dc. Turn.
Rep last 4 rows **1** (**2**-**3**-**6**) time(s) more. **42** (**46**-**50**-**54**) sts.

Cont even in pat until work from beg measures **11** (**12½**-**15**-**17½**) ins [**28** (**32**-**38**-**44.5**) cm], ending with a WS row. Break contrast colors.

With MC only:
Shape raglans: 1st row: (RS). Miss first **4** (**4**-**5**-**5**) dc. Join MC to next dc. Ch 1. 1 sc in same st as last sl st. 1 sc in each dc to last **4** (**4**-**5**-**5**) dc. **Turn.** Leave rem sts unworked. Cont on rem **34** (**38**-**40**-**44**) sts:
2nd row: Ch 3 (counts as dc). 1 dc in each sc to end of row. Turn.
3rd row: Ch 1. *Sc2tog. 1 sc in each dc to last 2 dc. Sc2tog. Turn.
Rep last 2 rows **1** (**2**-**2**-**2**) time(s) more. **30** (**32**-**34**-**38**) sts.

Next row: (WS). Ch 3 (counts as dc). Dc2tog made. 1 dc in each sc to last 3 sts. Dc2tog. 1 dc in last st. Turn.
Next row: Ch 1. Sc2tog. 1 sc in each dc to last 2 sts. Sc2tog. Turn.
Rep last 2 rows **4** (**4**-**4**-**5**) times more. **10** (**12**-**14**-**14**) sts.
Next row: (WS). Ch 3 (counts as dc). Dc2tog. 1 dc in each sc to last 3 sts. Dc2tog. 1 dc in last st. **8** (**10**-**12**-**12**) sts rem. Fasten off.

FINISHING
Sew raglan seams.

Hood: With RS facing, join MC to right front neck edge. Ch 1. 1 sc in each of next **25** (**27**-**30**-**32**) sc (including sts on top of sleeves) (1 sc in next sc. 2 sc in next sc) **11** (**12**-**13**-**14**) times (across back neck edge). 1 sc in each of next **26** (**28**-**30**-**33**) sc to corner of left front neck edge. Turn. **84** (**91**-**99**-**107**) sc in total.
Cont in Stripe Pat, proceed in pat as given for Back until Hood from 1st row measures **11** (**11**-**12**-**12**) ins [**28** (**28**-**30.5**-**30.5**) cm], ending with a WS row. Fasten off.
Sew top seam.
Sew Placket in position, overlapping right side over left side for Girl's Version or left side over right side for Boy's Version.

Front edging: With RS facing join MC with sl st to bottom of placket opening. Ch 1. Work 1 row of sc around placket opening and Hood. Fasten off. ♣

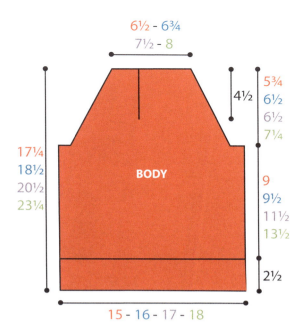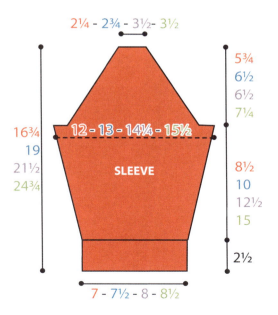

Joy Stripes Hoodie 11

2 Newsboy Set

EASY

SIZES

CAP

To fit head size		
6/8	20½ ins	[52 cm]
10/12	21½ ins	[54.5 cm]

MITTENS

To fit width around palm of hand		
6/8	6 ins	[15 cm]
10/12	6¾ ins	[17 cm]

TENSIONS

Cap: 14 sc and 15 rows = 4 ins [10 cm] with larger hook.

Mittens: 15½ sc and 16 rows = 4 ins [10 cm] with smaller hook.

MATERIALS

Patons® Canadiana (100 g/3.5 oz; 187 m /205 yds)				
CAP and MITTENS Sizes		6/8	10/12	
	10522 (Crantini)	2	3	**balls**
	or 10630 (Burnt Orange)			

Sizes 4 mm (U.S. G or 6) and 5 mm (U.S. H or 8) crochet hooks **or size needed to obtain tensions.**

STITCH GLOSSARY
See page 67 for Helpful Hints.
Beg = Beginning.
Ch = Chain(s).
Cont = Continue(ity).
Hdc = Half double crochet.
Rem = Remaining.
Rep = Repeat.
Rnd(s) = Round(s).
RS = Right side.
Sc = Single crochet.
Sl st = Slip stitch.
Sp(s) = Space(s).
St(s) = Stitch(es).
WS = Wrong side.
Yoh = Yarn over hook.

INSTRUCTIONS

The instructions are written for smaller size. If changes are necessary for larger size the instructions will be written thus ( ). Numbers for each size are shown in the same color throughout the pattern. When only one number is given in black, it applies to both sizes.

CAP

Note: Ch 2 at beg of rnd counts as hdc throughout.

With larger hook, ch 4. Join with sl st to first ch to form a ring.

1st rnd: Ch 2. 7 hdc in ring. Join with sl st to top of ch 2.

2nd rnd: Ch 2. 1 hdc in sp before next hdc. *2 hdc in sp between next 2 hdc. Rep from * around. Join with sl st to top of ch 2. 16 hdc.

3rd rnd: Ch 2. 1 hdc in sp before next hdc. *1 hdc in sp between next 2 hdc. 2 hdc in sp between next 2 hdc. Rep from * around, ending with 2 hdc in sp between last 2 hdc. Join with sl st to top of ch 2. 24 hdc.

4th rnd: Ch 2. 1 hdc in sp before next hdc. *2 hdc in sp between next 2 hdc. (1 hdc in sp between next 2 hdc) twice. Rep from * around, ending with 2 hdc in sp between last 2 hdc. Join with sl st to top of ch 2. 32 hdc.

5th rnd: Ch 2. 1 hdc in sp before next hdc. *2 hdc in sp between next 2 hdc. (1 hdc in sp between next 2 hdc) 3 times. Rep from * around, ending with 1 hdc in sp between last 2 hdc. Join with sl st to top of ch 2. 40 hdc.

6th rnd: Ch 2. 1 hdc in sp before next hdc. *(1 hdc in sp between next 2 hdc) 3 times. 2 hdc in sp between next 2 hdc. 1 hdc in sp between next 2 hdc. Rep from * around, ending with (1 hdc in sp between next 2 hdc) 4 times. 1 hdc in same sp as first hdc. Join with sl st to top of ch 2. 48 hdc.

7th rnd: Ch 2. 1 hdc in sp before next hdc. *1 hdc in sp between next 2 hdc. 2 hdc in sp between next 2 hdc. (1 hdc in sp between next 2 hdc) 4 times. Rep from * around, ending with (1 hdc in sp between next 2 hdc) twice. Join with sl st to top of ch 2. 56 hdc.

8th rnd: Ch 2. 1 hdc in sp before next hdc. *2 hdc in sp between next 2 hdc. (1 hdc in sp between next 2 hdc) 6 times. Rep from * around, ending with (1 hdc in sp between next 2 hdc) 4 times. Join with sl st to top of ch 2. 64 hdc.

9th rnd: Ch 2. 1 hdc in sp before next hdc. *(1 hdc in sp between next 2 hdc) 4 times. 2 hdc in sp between next 2 hdc. (1 hdc in sp between next 2 hdc) 3 times. Rep from * around, ending with 1 hdc in sp between last 2 hdc. Join with sl st to top of ch 2. 72 hdc.

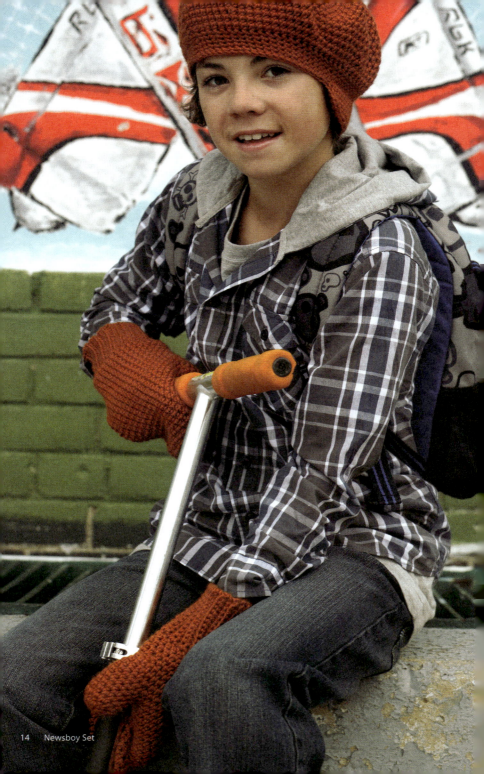

10th rnd: Ch 2. 1 hdc in sp before next hdc. *2 hdc in sp between next 2 hdc. (1 hdc in sp between next 2 hdc) 8 times. Rep from * around, ending with (1 hdc in sp between next 2 hdc) 6 times. Join with sl st to top of ch 2. 80 hdc.

11th rnd: Ch 2. 1 hdc in sp before next hdc. *(1 hdc in sp between next 2 hdc) 4 times. 2 hdc in sp between next 2 hdc. (1 hdc in sp between next 2 hdc) 5 times. Rep from * around, ending with (1 hdc in sp between next 2 hdc) 3 times. Join with sl st to top of ch 2. 88 hdc.

12th rnd: Ch 2. 1 hdc in sp before next hdc. *1 hdc in sp between next 2 hdc. Rep from * around. Join with sl st to top of ch 2.
Rep last rnd **6** (**8**) times more.

Shaping: 1st rnd: Ch 2. 1 hdc in sp before next hdc. *Yoh and draw up a loop in sp between next 2 hdc. Draw up a loop in sp between following 2 hdc. Yoh and draw through all 4 loops on hook – hdc2tog made. (1 hdc in sp between next 2 hdc) 9 times. Rep from * around, ending with (1 hdc in sp between next 2 hdc) 8 times. Join with sl st to top of ch 2. 80 sts.

2nd rnd: Ch 2. 1 hdc in sp before next hdc. *1 hdc in sp between next 2 hdc. Rep from * around. Join with sl st to top of ch 2.

3rd rnd: Ch 2. 1 hdc in sp before next hdc. (1 hdc in sp between next 2 hdc) 4 times. *Hdc2tog. (1 hdc in sp between next 2 hdc) **8** (**18**) times. Rep from * around, ending with (1 hdc in sp between next 2 hdc) **5** (**15**) times. Join with sl st to top of ch 2. **72** (**76**) sts.

Change to smaller hook.

Next rnd: Ch 1. Work 1 sc in each hdc around. Join with sl st to first sc. **72** (**76**) sc.

Next rnd: Ch 1. 1 sc in each sc around. Join with sl st to first sc.
Rep last rnd twice more. Fasten off.
Place markers on last rnd **19** (**21**) sts out from each side of joining st (center back). 34 sts between markers.

Brim: 1st rnd: (RS). With smaller hook, join yarn with sl st in **front loop only** of first st between markers. Ch 1. 1 sc in same sp. 1 sc in **front loop only** of each of next 33 sc. **Turn.** Leave rem sts unworked. With WS of Cap facing and working into rem loops of sts, work 1 sc in each of next 34 sc. Join with sl st to first sc. 68 sc.

2nd and 3rd rnds: Ch 1. 1 sc in each sc around. Join with sl st to first sc.

4th rnd: Ch 1. *Draw up a loop in each of next 2 sc. Yoh and draw through all 3 loops on hook* - sc2tog made. 1 sc in each of next 30 sc. (Sc2tog) twice. 1 sc in each of next 30 sc. Sc2tog. Join with sl st to first st.

5th rnd: Ch 1. Sc2tog. 1 sc in each of next 28 sc. (Sc2tog) twice. 1 sc in each of next 28 sc. Sc2tog. Join with sl st to first st. Fasten off.

Final rnd: (RS). Join yarn with sl st at center back of Cap. Ch 1. 1 sc in each of next **19** (**21**) sc. Work 6 sc up side of Brim. Work 30 sc across final edge of Brim (working through both thicknesses to join). Work 6 sc down side of Brim. 1 sc in each of next **19** (**21**) sc. Join with sl st to first sc. Fasten off.

MITTENS
LEFT MITTEN
**Cuff: (Worked sideways). With smaller hook, ch 13 leaving a long end.
1st row: (RS). 1 sc in 2nd ch from hook. 1 sc in each ch across. Turn. 12 sc.
2nd row: Ch 1. Working into **back loop only**, work 1 sc in each sc across. Turn.
Rep last row until Cuff (when slightly stretched) measures **6½** (**7**) ins [**16.5** (**18**) cm], ending with a WS row. **Do not** fasten off. Using yarn end from foundation ch, sew cuff seam.

Work rem of Mitten in rnds as follows:
1st rnd: Ch 1. Work **25** (**27**) sc evenly around top edge of Cuff. Join with sl st to first sc. Place a marker at end of last rnd.
Note: Ch 2 at beg of rnd counts as hdc throughout.
2nd rnd: Ch 2. 1 hdc in each sc around. Join with sl st to top of ch 2.
3rd and 4th rnds: Ch 2. 1 hdc in sp before next hdc. *1 hdc in sp between next 2 hdc. Rep from * around. Join with sl st to top of ch 2.**

Shape thumb gusset: 1st rnd: Ch 2. 1 hdc in sp before next hdc. (1 hdc in sp between next 2 hdc) **4** (**5**) times. 3 hdc in sp between next 2 hdc. *1 hdc in sp between next 2 hdc. Rep from * around. Join with sl st to top of ch 2. **27** (**29**) sts.
2nd rnd: Ch 2. 1 hdc in sp before next hdc. (1 hdc in sp between next 2 hdc) **5** (**6**) times. (2 hdc in sp between next 2 hdc) twice. *1 hdc in sp between next 2 hdc. Rep from * around. Join with sl st to top of ch 2. **29** (**31**) sts.
3rd rnd: Ch 2. 1 hdc in sp before next hdc. (1 hdc in sp between next 2 hdc) **5** (**6**) times. 2 hdc in sp between next 2 hdc. (1 hdc in sp between next 2 hdc) 3 times. 2 hdc in sp between next 2 hdc. *1 hdc in sp between next 2 hdc. Rep from * around. Join with sl st to top of ch 2. **31** (**33**) sts.
4th rnd: Ch 2. 1 hdc in sp before next hdc. (1 hdc in sp between next 2 hdc) **5** (**6**) times. 2 hdc in sp between next 2 hdc. (1 hdc in sp between next 2 hdc) 6 times. 2 hdc in sp between next 2 hdc. *1 hdc in sp between next 2 hdc. Rep from * around. Join with sl st to top of ch 2. **33** (**35**) sts.

Shape thumb opening: Next rnd: Ch 2. 1 hdc in sp before next hdc. (1 hdc in sp between next 2 hdc) **6** (**7**) times. Ch 1. Miss next 11 hdc. 1 hdc in sp between last missed hdc and next hdc. *1 hdc in sp between next 2 hdc. Rep from * around. Join with sl st to top of ch 2. **23** (**25**) sts.

Newsboy Set

***Next rnd:** Ch 2. 1 hdc in sp before next hdc. *1 hdc in sp between next 2 hdc. Rep from * around. Join with sl st to top of ch 2. Rep last rnd until work from marked rnd measures **5½** (**6¼**) ins [**14** (**16**) cm].

Shape top: 1st rnd: Ch 2. 1 hdc in sp before next hdc. *Yoh and draw up a loop in sp between next 2 hdc. Draw up a loop in sp between following 2 hdc. Yoh and draw through all 4 loops on hook – hdc2tog made. 1 hdc in sp between next 2 hdc. Rep from * around ending with (1 hdc in sp between next 2 hdc) **1** (**3**) time(s). Join with sl st to top of ch 2. **16** (**18**) sts.
2nd rnd: Ch 2. *(1 hdc in sp between next 2 hdc) **2** (**1**) time(s). Hdc2tog. Rep from * around. Join with sl st to top of ch 2. 12 sts.
3rd rnd: Ch 2. 1 hdc in sp before next hdc. *Hdc2tog. 1 hdc in sp between next 2 hdc. Rep from * around. Join with sl st to top of ch 2. 8 sts. Fasten off, leaving a long end. Turn Mitten inside out.
Joining row: (WS). Fold final rnd in half and with yarn end, ch 1. Working through both thicknesses, work 1 sc in each of next 4 sc. Fasten off.

Thumb: 1st rnd: (RS). Join yarn with sl st in ch-1 sp. Ch 2. (1 hdc in sp between next 2 hdc) 11 times. Join with sl st to top of ch 2. 12 sts
2nd to 5th rnds: Ch 2. 1 hdc in sp before next hdc. *1 hdc in sp between next 2 hdc. Rep from * around. Join with sl st to top of ch 2.
6th rnd: Ch 2. 1 hdc in sp before next hdc. *Hdc2tog. Rep from * around. Join with sl st to top of ch 2. Fasten off, leaving a long end. Draw end tightly through rem sts and fasten securely.***

RIGHT MITTEN

Work from ** to ** as given for Left Mitten.

Shape thumb gusset: 1st rnd: Ch 2. 1 hdc in sp before next hdc. (1 hdc in sp between next 2 hdc) **16** (**17**) times. 3 hdc in sp between next 2 hdc. *1 hdc in sp between next 2 hdc. Rep from * around. Join with sl st to top of ch 2. **27** (**29**) sts.
2nd rnd: Ch 2. 1 hdc in sp before next hdc. (1 hdc in sp between next 2 hdc) **16** (**17**) times. (2 hdc in sp between next 2 hdc) twice. *1 hdc in sp between next 2 hdc. Rep from * around. Join with sl st to top of ch 2. **29** (**31**) sts.

3rd rnd: Ch 2. 1 hdc in sp before next hdc. (1 hdc in sp between next 2 hdc) 17 (18) times. 2 hdc in sp between next 2 hdc. (1 hdc in sp between next 2 hdc) 3 times. 2 hdc in sp between next 2 hdc. *1 hdc in sp between next 2 hdc. Rep from * around. Join with sl st to top of ch 2. 31 (33) sts.

4th rnd: Ch 2. 1 hdc in sp before next hdc. (1 hdc in sp between next 2 hdc) 17 (18) times. 2 hdc in sp between next 2 hdc. (1 hdc in sp between next 2 hdc) 6 times. 2 hdc in sp between next 2 hdc. *1 hdc in sp between next 2 hdc. Rep from * around. Join with sl st to top of ch 2. 33 (35) sts.

Shape thumb opening: Next rnd: Ch 2. 1 hdc in sp before next hdc. (1 hdc in sp between next 2 hdc) 18 (19) times. Ch 1. Miss next 11 hdc. 1 hdc in sp between last missed hdc and next hdc. *1 hdc in sp between next 2 hdc. Rep from * around. Join with sl st to top of ch 2. 23 (25) sts.

Work from *** to *** as given for Left Mitten. ♣

3 Bobblicious Set

INTERMEDIATE

SIZES
MITTENS

To fit width around palm of hand		
6/8	6 ins	[15 cm]
10/12	6¾ ins	[17 cm]

COWL

Finished Size		
6/8	9½ x 11½ ins	[24 x 29 cm]
10/12	11 x 13½ ins	[28 x 34.5 cm]

MATERIALS

Patons® Canadiana (100 g/3.5 oz; 187 m /205 yds)					
COWL		Sizes	6/8	10/12	
	10704 (Tomato Red)		2	2	balls
MITTENS					
	10704 (Tomato Red)		1	1	ball

Cowl: Size 5 mm (U.S. 8) knitting needles **or size needed to obtain tension.** Cable needle.

Mittens: Sets of 4 sizes 3.75 mm (U.S. 5) and 4 mm (U.S. 6) double-pointed knitting needles **or size needed to obtain tension.** Cable needle. 1 stitch holder.

TENSIONS

Cowl: 19 sts and 25 rows = 4 ins [10 cm] with 5 mm (U.S. 8) needles in stocking st.

Mittens: 21 sts and 28 rows = 4 ins [10 cm] with 4 mm (U.S. 6) needles in stocking st.

STITCH GLOSSARY
See page 67 for Helpful Hints.
Alt = Alternate(ing).
Cont = Continue(ity).
C6B = Slip next 3 stitches onto a cable needle and leave at back of work. K3, then K3 from cable needle.
Inc 1P = Increase 1 stitch purlwise in next stitch by purling into front and back of next stitch.
K = Knit.
K2tog = Knit next 2 stitches together.
M1 = Make 1 stitch by picking up horizontal loop lying before next stitch and knitting into back of loop.

MB = **Make bobble**: Knit into front, back, and front of next st. (**Turn.** K3) 3 times. **Turn.** Sl1. K2tog. psso.
P = Purl.
P2tog = Purl next 2 stitches together.
Pat = Pattern.

Psso = Pass slipped stitch over.
Rem = Remaining.
Rep = Repeat.
Rnd(s) = Round(s).
RS = Right side.
Sl1 = Slip next stitch knitwise.
Ssk = Slip next 2 stitches knitwise one at a time. Pass them back onto left-hand needle, then knit through back loops together.
St(s) = Stitch(es).
Tog = Together.
T3B = Slip next stitch onto a cable needle and leave at back of work. K2, then P1 from cable needle.
T3F = Slip next 2 stitches onto a cable needle and leave at front of work. P1, then K2 from cable needle.
T5B = Slip next 3 stitches onto a cable needle and leave at back of work. K2, then P3 from cable needle.
T5F = Slip next 2 stitches onto a cable needle and leave at front of work. P3, then K2 from cable needle.
WS = Wrong side.

INSTRUCTIONS

The instructions are written for smaller size. If changes are necessary for larger size the instructions will be written thus ( ). Numbers for each size are shown in the same color throughout the pattern. When only one number is given in black, it applies to both sizes.

COWL

Cast on **107** (**122**) sts.
Knit 5 rows (garter st), noting first row is WS.

Next row: (RS). K1. *K2. M1. K3. M1. Rep from * to last st. K1. **149** (**170**) sts.
Next row: K1. *K4. P6. K6. P2. K3. Rep from * to last st. K1.

Proceed in Cable Bobble Pat as follows:
(See chart on page 25).
1st row: (RS). K1. *P3. T3B. P5. C6B. P4. Rep from * to last st. K1.
2nd row: K1. *K4. P6. K6. P2. K3. Rep from * to last st. K1.
3rd row: K1. *P2. T3B. P4. T5B. T5F. P2. Rep from * to last st. K1.

4th row: K1. *K2. P3. K4. P3. K5. P2. K2. Rep from * to last st. K1.
5th row: K1. *P1. T3B. P3. T5B. P4. T5F. Rep from * to last st. K1.
6th row: K1. *P3. K8. P3. K2. MB. K1. P2. K1. Rep from * to last st. K1.
7th row: K1. *P1. T3F. P3. K3. P8. K3. Rep from * to last st. K1.
8th row: K1. *P3. K8. P3. K3. P2. K2. Rep from * to last st. K1.
9th row: K1. *P2. T3F. P2. T5F. P4. T5B. Rep from * to last st. K1.
10th row: K1. *K2. (P3. K4) twice. P2. K3. Rep from * to last st. K1.
11th row: K1. *P3. T3F. P3. T5F. T5B. P2. Rep from * to last st. K1.
12th row: K1. *K4. P6. K5. P2. K1. MB. K2. Rep from * to last st. K1.
These 12 rows form Cable Bobble Pat.

Rep these 12 rows **4** (**5**) times more.
Next row: (RS). K1. *P4. K6. P5. K2. P4. Rep from * to last st. K1.
Next row: K1. *K1. K2tog. K2. K2tog. Rep from * to last st. K1. **107** (**122**) sts.
Knit 5 rows (garter st).
Cast off knitwise (WS). Sew side seam.

MITTENS

Cable Panel (worked over 14 sts).
(See chart on page 25)
1st row: P4. C6B. P4.
2nd row: P4. K6. P4.
3rd row: P2. T5B. T5F. P2.
4th row: P2. K3. P4. K3. P2.
5th row: T5B. P4. T5F.
6th to 8th rows: K3. P8. K3.
9th row: T5F. P4. T5B.
10th row: P2. K3. P4. K3. P2.
11th row: P2. T5F. T5B. P2.
12 row: MB. P3. K6. P3. MB.
These 12 rows form Cable Panel.

RIGHT MITTEN

***Cuff:** With set of 4 smaller double-pointed needles, cast on **32** (**36**) sts. Divide sts onto 3 needles as follows: **11,11,10** (**12,12,12**) sts. Join in rnd, placing marker on first st.
Work in (K2. P2) ribbing for 3 ins [7.5 cm].

Next rnd: *P**8** (**9**). M1. Rep from * to end of rnd. **36** (**40**) sts.
Change to set of 4 larger double-pointed needles. **
1st rnd: P**3** (**4**). Work 1st row of Cable Panel. Purl to end of rnd.
2nd rnd: P**3** (**4**). Work 2nd row of Cable Panel. Purl to end of rnd.
Cable Panel is now in position. Work a further 7 rnds in pat.

Shape thumb gusset: 1st rnd: Pat across next **19** (**21**) sts. (Inc 1P in next st) twice. Purl to end of rnd.
2nd and alt rnds: Work even in pat.
3rd rnd: Pat across next **19** (**21**) sts. Inc 1P in next st. P2. Inc 1P in next st. Purl to end of rnd.

5th rnd: Pat across next **19** (**21**) sts. Inc 1P in next st. P4. Inc 1P in next st. Purl to end of rnd.
7th rnd: Pat across next **19** (**21**) sts. Inc 1P in next st. P6. Inc 1P in next st. Purl to end of rnd.
9th rnd: Pat across next **19** (**21**) sts. Inc 1P in next st. P8. Inc 1P in next st. Pat to end of rnd. **46** (**50**) sts.
10th rnd: Pat across next **19** (**21**) sts. Slip next 12 sts onto st holder. Cast on 2 sts. Purl to end of rnd. **36** (**40**) sts.

***Cont even in pat until 36 rnds in total of Cable Panel have been completed, ending with a 12th row of Cable Panel.
Next rnd: P**3** (**4**). ssk. P3. ssk. K2tog. P3. K2tog. Purl to end of rnd. **32** (**36**) sts.

Size 10/12 only: Purl 6 rnds.

Both sizes: Rearrange sts over 3 needles as follows: **16**, **8**, **8** (**18**, **9**, **9**) sts.

Shape top: 1st rnd: *1st needle:* P1. P2tog. Purl to last 3 sts. P2tog. P1. *2nd needle:* P1. P2tog. Purl to end of needle. *3rd needle:* Purl to last 3 sts. P2tog. P1.
2nd and alt rnds: Purl.
Rep last 2 rnds until 16 sts rem. Divide sts onto 2 needles. Graft 2 groups of 8 sts tog.

Make thumb: P12 from st holder. Pick up and purl 2 sts at base of thumb. Join in rnd. 14 sts. Divide sts evenly onto 3 needles (5, 4, 5) sts. Purl in rnds for **1¾** (**2**) ins [**4.5** (**5**) cm].

Next rnd: *P2tog. Rep from * around. Break yarn. Thread end through rem 7 sts. Draw up tightly and fasten securely. ***

LEFT MITTEN

Work from ** to ** as given for Right Mitten.

1st rnd: P**19** (**22**). Work 1st row of Cable Panel. Purl to end of rnd.
2nd rnd: P**19** (**22**). Work 2nd row of Cable Panel. Purl to end of rnd.
Cable Panel is now in position. Work a further 7 rnds in Pat.

Shape thumb gusset: 1st rnd: P**15** (**17**). (Inc 1P in next st) twice. Pat to end of rnd.
2nd and alt rnds: Work even in pat.
3rd rnd: P**15** (**17**). Inc 1P in next st. P2. Inc 1P in next st. Pat to end of rnd.
5th rnd: P**15** (**17**). Inc 1P in next st. P4. Inc 1P in next st. Pat to end of rnd.
7th rnd: P**15** (**17**). Inc 1P in next st. P6. Inc 1P in next st. Purl to end of rnd.
9th rnd: P**15** (**17**). Inc 1P in next st. P8. Inc 1P in next st. Purl to end of rnd. **46** (**50**) sts.
10th rnd: P**15** (**17**). Slip next 12 sts onto st holder. Cast on 2 sts. Pat to end of rnd. **32** (**36**) sts.

Work from *** to *** as given for Right Mitten. ♦

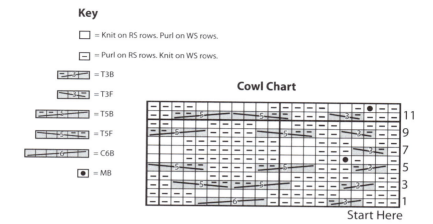

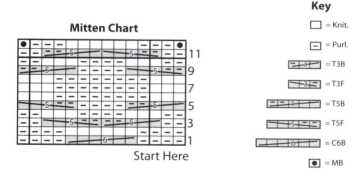

Pattern Ratings

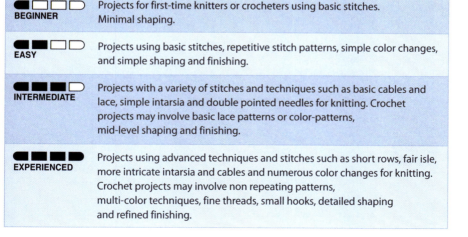

Bobblicious Set 25

4 Coco Cropped Cardigan

EASY

SIZES

To fit chest measurement		
6	25 ins	[63.5 cm]
8	26½ ins	[67.5 cm]
10	28 ins	[71 cm]
12	30 ins	[76 cm]

Finished chest		
6	28 ins	[71 cm]
8	30 ins	[76 cm]
10	33 ins	[84 cm]
12	34½ ins	[87.5 cm]

TENSION

14 hdc and 9 rows = 4 ins [10 cm].

MATERIALS

Patons® Canadiana (100 g/3.5 oz; 187 m /205 yds)					
Sizes	6	8	10	12	
Main Color (MC) 10413 (Raspberry)	2	3	3	4	balls
Contrast A 10430 (Burgundy)	1	1	1	1	ball

Size 5 mm (U.S. H or 8) crochet hook **or size needed to obtain tension.** 3 snap fasteners.

> **STITCH GLOSSARY**
> See page 67 for Helpful Hints.
> **Beg** = Beginning.
> **Ch(s)** = Chain(s).
> **Cont** = Continue(ity).
> **Dc** = Double crochet.
> **Hdc** = Half double crochet.
> **Rem** = Remain(ing).
> **Rep** = Repeat.
> **Rnd(s)** = Round(s).
> **RS** = Right side.
> **Sc** = Single crochet.
> **Sl st** = Slip stitch.
> **Sp** = Space.
> **St(s)** = Stitch(es).
> **WS** = Wrong side.
> **Yoh** = Yarn over hook.

INSTRUCTIONS

The instructions are written for smallest size. If changes are necessary for larger sizes the instructions will be written thus ( ). Numbers for each size are shown in the same color throughout the pattern. When only one number is given in black, it applies to all sizes.

Notes: Body is worked in one piece to armholes.
Ch 2 at beg of row does not count as hdc throughout.

BODY

With MC, ch **100** (**110**-**118**-**124**) **loosely.**
1st row: (RS). 1 hdc in 3rd ch from hook. 1 hdc in each ch to end of ch. Turn. **98** (**108**-**116**-**122**) hdc.
2nd row: Ch 2. *Working in front loops only,* 1 hdc in each hdc to end of row. Turn.
3rd row: Ch 2. *Working in back loops only,* 1 hdc in each hdc to end of row. Turn.
Rep last 2 rows until piece from beg measures **4** (**4½**-**5½**-**7½**) ins [**10** (**11.5**-**14**-**19**) cm], ending with a WS.

Divide for armholes:
Right Front: 1st row: (RS). Ch 2. *Working in back loops only,* 1 hdc in each of next **22** (**23**-**24**-**25**) hdc. **Turn.** Leave rem sts unworked.
2nd row: Ch 2. *Working in front loops only,* 1 hdc in each hdc to end of row. Turn.
3rd row: Ch 2. *Working in back loops only,* 1 hdc in each hdc to end of row. Turn.
Rep last 2 rows until armhole divide measures **4** (**4½**-**4½**-**5**) ins [**10** (**11.5**-**11.5**-**12.5**) cm], ending with a WS row.

Shape neck: 1st row: (RS). Sl st in each of next **5** (**5**-**6**-**6**) hdc. Ch 2. *Working in back loops only,* 1 hdc in each hdc to end of row. Turn. **17** (**18**-**18**-**19**) hdc.
2nd row: Ch 2. *Working in front loops only,* 1 hdc in each hdc to last 2 hdc. *Yoh and draw up a loop in each of next 2 hdc. Yoh and draw through all loops on hook* - hdc2tog made. Turn. **16** (**17**-**17**-**18**) sts.
3rd row: Ch 2. *Working in back loops only,* 1 hdc in each st to end of row. Turn.
Rep last 2 rows **1** (**1**-**2**-**2**) time(s) more. **15** (**16**-**15**-**16**) sts.
Work 1 row even. Fasten off.

Back: 1st row: (RS). Miss next **5** (**8**-**10**-**11**) hdc. Join MC with sl st to next unworked hdc. Ch 2. *Working in back loops only,* 1 hdc in same sp as last sl st. 1 hdc in each of next **43** (**45**-**47**-**49**) hdc. **Turn.** Leave rem hdc unworked.
2nd row: Ch 2. *Working in front loops only,* 1 hdc in each hdc across. Turn.
3rd row: Ch 2. *Working in back loops only,* 1 hdc in each hdc across. Turn.
Rep last 2 rows until armhole measures same length as Front. Fasten off.

Left Front: 1st row: (RS). Miss next **5** (**8**-**10**-**11**) hdc. Join MC with sl st to next unworked hdc. Ch 2. *Working in back loops only,* 1 hdc in same sp as last sl st. 1 hdc in each hdc across. Turn. **22** (**23**-**24**-**25**) hdc.
2nd row: Ch 2. *Working in front loops only,* 1 hdc in each hdc across. Turn.
Rep last 2 rows until armhole measures **4** (**4½**-**4½**-**5**) ins [**10** (**11.5**-**11.5**-**12.5**) cm], ending with a WS row.

Shape neck: 1st row: (RS). Ch 2. *Working in back loops only,* 1 hdc in each hdc to last **5** (**5**-**6**-**6**) hdc. **Turn.** Leave rem sts unworked. **17** (**18**-**18**-**19**) hdc.
2nd row: Ch 2. *Working in front loops only,* hdc2tog. 1 hdc in each hdc to end of row. Turn. **16** (**17**-**17**-**18**) sts.
3rd row: Ch 2. *Working in back loops only,* 1 hdc in each st to end of row. Turn.
Rep last 2 rows **1** (**1**-**2**-**2**) time(s) more. **15** (**16**-**15**-**16**) sts.
Work 1 row even. Fasten off.

SLEEVES

With MC, ch **41** (**45**-**49**-**52**) **loosely.**
1st row: (RS). 1 hdc in 3rd ch from hook. 1 hdc in each ch to end of ch. **39** (**43**-**47**-**50**) hdc.
2nd row: Ch 2. *Working in front loops only,* 1 hdc in each hdc to end of row. Turn.
3rd row: Ch 2. *Working in back loops only,* 2 hdc in first hdc. 1 hdc in each hdc to last hdc. 2 hdc in last hdc. Turn.
4th row: As 2nd row.
5th row: Ch 2. *Working in back loops only,* 1 hdc in each hdc to end of row. Turn.
Rep last 4 rows twice more. **45** (**49**-**53**-**56**) hdc.
Cont even in pat until Sleeve from beg measures **5½** (**6**-**6½**-**7**) ins [**14** (**15**-**16.5**-**18**) cm]. Fasten off.

Sleeve edging: 1st row: With RS facing, join MC to rem loop of foundation ch. Ch 1. 1 sc in each rem loop of foundation ch to end of row. Turn. **39** (**43**-**47**-**50**) sc.
2nd row: Ch 3 (counts as dc). 1 dc in each of next **1** (**0**-**2**-**0**) sc. *Miss next 2 sc. (3 dc. Ch 3. 3 dc) in next sc. Miss next 2 sc. 1 dc in next sc. Rep from * to last **1** (**0**-**2**-**1**) sc. 1 dc in each of last **1** (**0**-**2**-**1**) sc. Turn.
3rd row: Ch 3 (counts as dc). 1 dc in each of next **1** (**0**-**2**-**1**) dc. *(3 dc. Ch 3. 3 dc) in next ch-3 sp. 1 dc in next dc. Rep from * to last **1** (**0**-**2**-**0**) dc. 1 dc in each of last **1** (**0**-**2**-**0**) dc. Turn.

4th row: Ch 3 (counts as dc). 1 dc in each of next **1** (**0**-**2**-**0**) dc. *(3 dc. Ch 3. 3 dc) in next ch-3 sp. 1 dc in next dc. Rep from * to last **1** (**0**-**2**-**1**) dc. 1 dc in each of last **1** (**0**-**2**-**1**) dc. Turn.

5th row: Ch 1. *1 sc in each dc to next ch-3 sp. (2 sc. Ch 4. Sl st in first ch. 2 sc) in next ch-3 sp. Rep from * to end of row, ending with 1 sc in each of last **5** (**4**-**6**-**5**) dc. Fasten off.

FINISHING

Pin garment pieces to measurements. Cover with a damp cloth, leaving cloth to dry.
Sew shoulder and sleeve seams. Sew in sleeves.

Edging: 1st row: With RS facing, join A with sl st to top of Right Front edge. Ch 1. Work **28** (**32**-**36**-**44**) sc evenly down Right Front edge. 3 sc in corner. Work 1 sc in each rem loop of bottom edge. 3 sc in corner. Work **28** (**32**-**36**-**44**) sc evenly up Left Front edge. **Do not** turn.

2nd row: Ch 1. Working from **left** to right instead of from **right** to left as usual, work 1 reverse sc in each sc to end of row. Fasten off.

Reverse sc diagram

COLLAR

With A, ch 9.

1st row: (RS). 1 sc in 2nd ch from hook. 1 sc in each ch to end of ch. Turn. 8 sc.

2nd row: Ch 1. 1 sc in each sc across. Turn. Rep last row until Collar, when slightly stretched, measures length to fit along neck edge. Fasten off.

Join A with sl st to bottom of side edge of Collar. Ch 1. Work 1 row of sc evenly up side edge, across top of Collar and down opposite side edge, having 3 sc in corners. **Do not** turn. Working from **left** to right instead of from **right** to left as usual, work 1 reverse sc in each sc to end of row. Fasten off. Sew Collar along neck edge.

BUTTONS (make 2).

With MC, ch 4. Join with sl st to form ring.

1st rnd: Ch 1. 6 sc in ring. Join with sl st to first sc.

2nd rnd: Ch 1. 2 sc in each sc around. Join A with sl st to first sc. 12 sc.

3rd rnd: With A, ch 1. 2 sc in first sc. *1 long dc in center of ring. Miss next sc. 2 sc in next sc. Rep from * to last sc. 1 long dc in center of ring. Miss last sc. Join with sl st to first sc. 18 sts.

4th rnd: Ch 1. 1 sc in each st around. Join with sl st to first sc. Fasten off.

Try on Cardigan. Mark placement for snap fasteners on front and Collar. Sew Buttons to Right Front on top of snap fasteners.

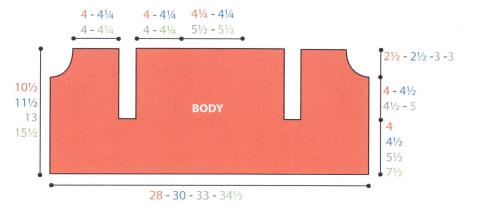

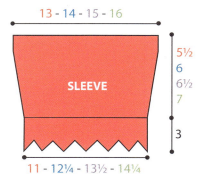

5 Super Stripes Jacket

EASY

SIZES

To fit chest measurement		
6	25 ins	[63.5 cm]
8	26½ ins	[67.5 cm]
10	28 ins	[71 cm]
12	30 ins	[76 cm]

Finished chest		
6	30 ins	[76 cm]
8	32 ins	[81.5 cm]
10	34 ins	[86.5 cm]
12	36 ins	[91.5 cm]

TENSION

20 sts and 26 rows = 4 ins [10 cm] with larger needles in stocking st.

STITCH GLOSSARY
See page 67 for Helpful Hints.
Beg = Beginning.
Cont = Continue(ity).
Inc = Increase 1 stitch into next stitch by knitting into front and back of next stitch.
K = Knit.
K2tog = Knit next 2 stitches together.
P = Purl.
P2tog = Purl next 2 stitches together.
P2togtbl = Purl next 2 stitches together through back loops.
Pat = Pattern.
Rem = Remaining.
Rep = Repeat.
Rnd(s) = Round(s).
RS = Right side.
Ssk = Slip next 2 stitches knitwise one at a time. Pass them back onto left-hand needle, then knit through back loops together.
St(s) = Stitch(es).
WS = Wrong side.

MATERIALS

Patons® Canadiana (100 g/3.5 oz; 187 m /205 yds)

GIRL'S VERSION	Sizes	6	8	10	12	
	Main Color (MC) 10044 (Med Grey Mix)	4	4	5	6	balls
	Contrast A 10712 (Lime Juice)	1	1	1	1	ball
	Contrast B 10008 (Aran)	1	1	1	1	ball
	Contrast C 10732 (Bubble Gum)	1	1	1	1	ball
	Contrast D 10332 (Deep Orchid)	1	1	1	1	ball

Patons® Canadiana (100 g/3.5 oz; 187 m /205 yds)

BOY'S VERSION	Sizes	6	8	10	12	
	Main Color (MC) 10012 (Toasty Grey)	4	4	5	6	balls
	Contrast A 10013 (Timber)	1	1	1	1	ball
	Contrast B 10022 (Oatmeal)	1	1	1	1	ball
	Contrast C 10145 (Dark Water Blue)	1	1	1	1	ball
	Contrast D 10630 (Burnt Orange)	1	1	1	1	ball

Sizes 4 mm (U.S. 6) and 4.5 mm (U.S. 7) circular knitting needles 36 ins [90 cm] long. Sets of four sizes 4 mm (U.S. 6) and 4.5 mm (U.S. 7) double-pointed knitting needles **or size needed to obtain tension.** Separating zipper.

INSTRUCTIONS

The instructions are written for smallest size. If changes are necessary for larger sizes the instructions will be written thus ( ). Numbers for each size are shown in the same color throughout the pattern. When only one number is given in black, it applies to all sizes.

Stripe Pat (worked in stocking st).
With MC, work 2 rows.
With B, work 1 row.
With A, work 4 rows.
With B, work 1 row.
With C, work 4 rows.
With B, work 1 row.
With D, work 4 rows.
With B, work 1 row.
With C, work 4 rows.
With B, work 1 row.
With A, work 4 rows.
With B, work 1 row.
With MC, work 4 rows.
With B, work 1 row.
With MC, work 4 rows.
With B, work 1 row.
These 38 rows form Stripe Pat.

BODY

With smaller circular needle and D, cast on **146** (**154**-**166**-**174**) sts. **Do not** join. Working back and forth across needle in rows, proceed as follows:
1st row: (RS). K2. *P2. K2. Rep from * to end of row.
2nd row: P2. *K2. P2. Rep from * to end of row.
Rep last 2 rows of (K2. P2) ribbing for 2½ ins [6 cm], inc **4** (**6**-**4**-**6**) sts evenly across last row and ending with a 2nd row. **150** (**160**-**170**-**180**) sts. Break D.

Change to larger circular needle and with B, work 2 rows stocking st. Break B.
With MC, cont in stocking st until work from beg measures **10** (**10½**-**12½**-**14½**) ins [**25.5** (**26.5**-**32**-**37**) cm], ending with a purl row.

Proceed as follows:
Next row: (RS). With B, knit.
With MC, work 4 rows stocking st.
Next row: With B, purl.
With MC, work 4 rows stocking st.
Next row: With B, knit. Break B.
Next row: With MC, purl.

Divide for Fronts and Back: 1st row: (RS). With MC, K**35** (**36**-**39**-**40**). Cast off **6** (**8**-**8**-**10**) sts. K**68** (**72**-**76**-**80**). Cast off **6** (**8**-**8**-**10**) sts. Knit to end of row. **Do not** break MC. Leave all sts on a needle.

SLEEVES

With smaller double-pointed needles and D, cast on **40** (**40**-**44**-**48**) sts. Divide sts onto 3 needles. Join in rnd placing marker on first st.

1st rnd: *K2. P2. Rep from * around.
Rep last rnd of (K2. P2) ribbing for 2½ ins [6 cm], inc **0** (**2**-**2**-**0**) sts evenly around last rnd. **40** (**42**-**46**-**48**) sts. Break D.

Change to larger double-pointed needles and with B, knit 2 rnds. Break B.
Proceed as follows:
1st rnd: With MC. Inc 1 st in first st. Knit to 2 last sts. Inc 1 st in next st. K1.
Knit **5** (**6**-**7**-**7**) rnds even.
Rep last **6** (**7**-**8**-**8**) rnds **7** (**8**-**9**-**10**) times more. **56** (**60**-**66**-**70**) sts.
Knit in rnds until work from beg measures **9½** (**11**-**13½**-**15**) ins [**24** (**28**-**34.5**-**38**) cm].

Proceed as follows:
1st rnd: With B, knit.
With MC, knit 4 rnds.
Rep last 5 rnds once more.
Next rnd: With B, knit. Break B.
Next rnd: With MC, knit to last **3** (**4**-**4**-**5**) sts. Cast off last **3** (**4**-**4**-**5**) sts.
Next rnd: Cast off next **3** (**4**-**4**-**5**) sts. Knit to end of rnd. **50** (**52**-**58**-**60**) sts. Break MC. Leave sts on a spare needle.

YOKE

With RS facing, MC and larger circular needle, K**35** (**36**-**39**-**40**) from Left Front. K**50** (**52**-**58**-**60**) from Left Sleeve. K**68** (**72**-**76**-**80**) from Back. K**50** (**52**-**58**-**60**) from Right Sleeve. K**35** (**36**-**39**-**40**) from Right Front. **238** (**248**-**270**-**280**) sts for Yoke.

Beg working in Stripe Pat, shape Yoke as follows:
1st row: (RS). K**33** (**34**-**37**-**38**). ssk. Place marker. K2tog. K**46** (**48**-**54**-**56**). ssk. Place marker. K2tog. K**64** (**68**-**72**-**76**). ssk. Place marker. K2tog. K**46** (**48**-**54**-**56**). ssk. Place marker. K2tog. **230** (**240**-**262**-**272**) sts.
2nd row: Purl.
3rd row: *Knit to 2 sts before marker. ssk. K2tog. Rep from * 3 times more. Knit to end of row.
Rep last 2 rows **13** (**13**-**15**-**18**) times more. **118** (**128**-**134**-**120**) sts rem.
Next row: (WS). Purl.

Note: When Stripe Pat is complete, work with MC only in stocking st.

Shape neck: 1st row: (RS). Cast off **6** (**6**-**7**-**7**) sts. *Knit to 2 sts before marker. ssk. K2tog. Rep from * 3 times more. Knit to end of row. **104** (**114**-**119**-**105**) sts rem.
2nd row: Cast off **6** (**6**-**7**-**7**) sts. Purl to end of row. **98** (**108**-**112**-**98**) sts rem.
3rd row: ssk. *Knit to 2 sts before marker. ssk. K2tog. Rep from * 3 times more. Knit to last 2 sts. K2tog.
4th row: P2tog. Purl to last 2 sts. P2togtbl. Rep last 2 rows once more, then 3rd row once. **64** (**74**-**78**-**64**) sts rem.

Size 6 only: Next row: (WS). *Purl to 2 sts before marker. P2tog. P2togtbl. Rep from * 3 times more. Purl to end of row.

Next row: *Knit to 2 sts before marker. ssk. K2tog. Rep from * 3 times more. Knit to end of row.
Next row: P2tog. P2togtbl. *Purl to 2 sts before marker. P2tog. P2togtbl. Rep from * twice more. 40 sts.

Sizes 8 and 10 only: 1st row: (WS). Purl.
2nd row: *Knit to 2 sts before marker. ssk. K2tog. Rep from * 3 times more. Knit to end of row.
3rd row: *Purl to 2 sts before marker. P2tog. P2togtbl. Rep from * 3 times more. Purl to end of row.
4th row: As 2nd row.
5th row: P2tog. P2togtbl. *Purl to 2 sts before marker. P2tog. P2togtbl. Rep from * twice more. (**42**-**46**) sts.

Size 12 only: 1st row: (RS). *Knit to 2 sts before marker. ssk. K2tog. Rep from * 3 times more. Knit to end of row.
2nd row: Purl.
3rd row: ssk. K2tog. *Knit to 2 sts before marker. ssk. K2tog. Rep from * once more. ssk. K2tog. 48 sts.
4th row: Purl.

FINISHING

Pin garment to measurements. Cover with a damp cloth, leaving cloth to dry.

Collar: With RS facing, smaller circular needle and MC, pick up and knit **21** (**21**-**23**-**23**) sts up right front neck edge. K**40** (**42**-**46**-**48**) sts across sleeve and back neck edge, dec **0** (**2**-**2**-**0**) sts evenly across. Pick up and knit **21** (**21**-**23**-**23**) sts down left front neck edge. **82** (**82**-**90**-**94**) sts.

Beg with 2nd row, work in (K2. P2) ribbing as given for Body for 2 ins [5 cm], ending with a 2nd row.
Next 2 rows: (fold edge). With B, knit.
With D, work in (K2. P2) ribbing for 2 ins [5 cm], ending with a 2nd row. Cast off.

Front edging: With RS facing, smaller circular needle and MC, pick up and knit **84** (**88**-**102**-**116**) sts along front edge between bottom edge and fold edge of Collar. Cast off. Rep for other side.

Sew zipper under front edging, ending at fold edge.
Fold Collar to WS along fold edge. Sew in position.
Sew underarm seams.

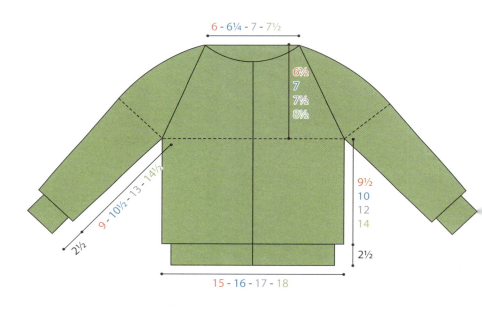

6 Bright and Slouchy Set

EASY

MEASUREMENTS

Scarf: Approx 7 ins [18 cm] wide x 70 ins [178 cm] long.
Hat: To fit child's head age **6/8** (**10/12**).

TENSIONS

14 hdc and 9 rows = 4 ins [10 cm].
Scarf Motif = 7 ins [18 cm] square.
Hat Motif = 4¼ ins [11 cm] square.

MATERIALS

Patons® Canadiana (100 g/3.5 oz; 187 m /205 yds)		
Main Color (MC) 10744 (Medium Teal)	2	**balls**
Contrast A 10307 (Grape Jelly)	1	**ball**
Contrast B 10320 (Cherished Lavender)	2	**balls**
Contrast C 10013 (Timber)	1	**ball**
Contrast D 10008 (Aran)	1	**ball**

Size 5 mm (U.S. H or 8) crochet hook **or size needed to obtain tension.**

STITCH GLOSSARY

See page 67 for Helpful Hints.
Alt = Alternate(ing).
Beg = Beginning.
Ch(s) = Chain(s).
Cont = Continue(ity).
Dc = Double crochet.
Dec = Decrease.
Hdc = Half double crochet.
Rem = Remain(ing).
Rep = Repeat.
Rnd(s) = Round(s).
RS = Right side.
Sc = Single crochet.
Sl st = Slip stitch.
Sp(s) = Space(s).
St(s) = Stitch(es).
Tog = Together.
Yoh = Yarn over hook.

INSTRUCTIONS

The instructions are written for smaller size. If changes are necessary for larger size the instructions will be written thus ( ). Numbers for each size are shown in the same color throughout the pattern. When only one number is given in black, it applies to both sizes.

SCARF

Motif (See chart on page 44).
With Color 1, ch 4. Join with sl st to form ring.

1st rnd: Ch 5 (counts as 1 dc. Ch 2). (3 dc. Ch 2) 3 times into ring. 2 dc. Join with sl st to 3rd ch of ch 5.

2nd rnd: Sl st in next ch-2 sp. Ch 7 (counts as 1 dc. Ch 4). 2 dc in same sp as last sl st. *1 dc in each dc to next ch-2 sp.** (2 dc. Ch 4. 2 dc) in next ch-2 sp. Rep from * twice, then from * to ** once more. 1 dc in next ch-2 sp. Join with sl st to 3rd ch of ch 7. Break Color 1.

3rd rnd: Join Color 2 with sl st to any corner ch-4 sp. Ch 7 (counts as 1 dc. Ch 4). 2 dc in same sp as last sl st. *1 dc in each dc to next ch-2 sp.**(2 dc. Ch 4. 2 dc) in next corner ch-4 sp. Rep from * twice, then from * to ** once more. 1 dc in next ch-4 sp. Join with sl st to 3rd ch of ch 7. Break Color 2.

4th and 5th rnds: Join Color 3 with sl st to any corner ch-4 sp. Ch 7 (counts as 1 dc. Ch 4). 2 dc in same sp as last sl st. *1 dc in each dc to next corner ch-4 sp.** (2 dc. Ch 4. 2 dc) in next corner ch-4 sp. Rep from * twice, then from * to ** once more. 1 dc in next ch-4 sp. Join with sl st to 3rd ch of ch 7. Break Color 3 at end of 5th rnd.

6th rnd: Join Color 4 with sl st to any corner ch-4 sp. Ch 1. (2 sc. Ch 2. 2 sc) in same ch-4 sp as last sl st. *1 sc in each dc to next corner ch-4 sp. (2 sc. Ch 2. 2 sc) in next corner ch-4 sp. Rep from * around. Break Color 4. Join Color 5 with sl st to first sc.

7th rnd: With Color 5, ch 1. 1 sc in each sc around, having 3 sc in each corner ch-2 sp. Join with sl st to first sc. Fasten off.

Motif 1
Make 5 Motifs having C as Color 1, MC as Color 2, A as Color 3, B as Color 4 and D as Color 5.

Motif 2
Make 5 Motifs having A as Color 1, B as Color 2, MC as Color 3, C as Color 4, and D as Color 5.

FINISHING

With D join 10 Motifs alternating Motif 1 and Motif 2.

Cut 8 inch [20.5 cm] lengths of yarn. Taking 8 strands tog, knot into fringe across ends of Scarf. Make 2 in each of MC, C and D. Make 4 each in A and B.

HAT

Motif [make **6** (**7**)] (See chart on page 44).
With C, ch 4. Join with sl st to form ring.
1st rnd: Ch 5 (counts as 1 dc. Ch 2). (3 dc. Ch 2) 3 times into ring. 2 dc. Join with sl st to 3rd ch of ch 5. Break C.
2nd rnd: Join D with sl st to any corner ch-2 sp. Ch 6 (counts as 1 dc. Ch 3). 2 dc in same sp as last sl st. *1 dc in each dc to next ch-2 sp.** (2 dc. Ch 3. 2 dc) in next ch-2 sp. Rep from * twice, then from * to ** once more. 1 dc in next ch-2 sp. Join A with sl st to 3rd ch of ch 6. Break D.
3rd rnd: With A, ch 1. Work 1 sc in each dc around, having 3 sc in each corner ch-4 sp. Join with sl st to first sc. Fasten off.

Join Motifs to form a strip. Sew ends of strip tog.
Note: Ch 2 at beg of rnd does not count as hdc throughout.

With RS facing, join MC with sl st to any sc along side edge of strip.
1st rnd: Ch 2. Work **60** (**70**) hdc evenly around (10 hdc across each Motif). Join with sl st to first hdc.
2nd rnd: Ch 2. 1 hdc in each hdc around. Join with sl st to first hdc.
Rep last rnd until work from top of Motif band measures 2½ ins [6 cm].

Size 6/8 only: Ch 2. *1 hdc in each of next 13 hdc. (*Yoh and draw up a loop in next hdc*) twice. Yoh and draw through all loops on hook – hdc2tog made. Rep from * around. Join with sl st to first hdc. 56 sts.

Size 10/12 only: Ch 2. 1 hdc in each of next 13 hdc. (*Yoh and draw up a loop in next hdc*) twice. Yoh and draw through all loops on hook – hdc2tog made. *1 hdc in each of next 9 hdc. Hdc2tog. Rep from * 4 times more. Join with sl st to first hdc. 64 sts.

Both sizes: Shape top: 1st rnd: Ch 2. 1 hdc in each st around. Join with sl st to first hdc.
2nd rnd: Ch 2. *1 hdc in each of next **5** (**6**) hdc. Hdc2tog. Rep from * around. Join with sl st to first hdc. **48** (**56**) sts.
3rd rnd: As 1st rnd.
4th rnd: Ch 2. *1 hdc in each of next **4** (**5**) hdc. Hdc2tog. Rep from * around. Join with sl st to first hdc. **40** (**48**) sts.
5th rnd: As 1st rnd.
6th rnd: Ch 2. *1 hdc in each of next **3** (**4**) hdc. Hdc2tog. Rep from * around. Join with sl st to first hdc. **32** (**40**) sts.
7th rnd: As 1st rnd.
Cont as established, dec 8 sts on next and every alt rnd to 8 sts.
Break yarn, leaving a long end. Thread end through rem loops and fasten securely.

Bottom edge: Join MC with sl st to sc at center back of bottom edge. Ch 1. Work **60** (**70**) sc evenly around (10 sc across each Motif). Join with sl st to first sc.
Fasten off. ♣

Hat Motif

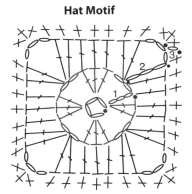

Key

- • = slip stitch (sl st)
- ⌒ = chain (ch)
- + = single crochet (sc)
- T = double crochet (dc)

Scarf Motif

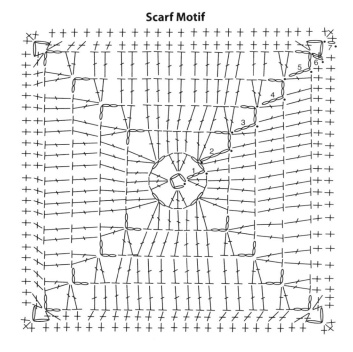

7a Rosey Band

EASY

SIZES

Finished circumference		
6/8	16 ins	[40.5 cm]
10/12	18 ins	[45.5 cm]

TENSION

14 hdc and 9 rows = 4 ins [10 cm].

MATERIALS

Patons® Canadiana (100 g/3.5 oz; 187 m /205 yds)				
	Sizes	6/8	10/12	
	Main Color (MC) 10430 (Burgundy)	1	1	ball
	Contrast A 10413 (Raspberry)	1	1	ball

Size 5 mm (U.S. H or 8) crochet hook **or size needed to obtain tension.**

STITCH GLOSSARY
See page 67 for Helpful Hints.
Beg = Beginning.
Ch(s) = Chain(s).
Dc = Double crochet.
Hdc = Half double crochet.
Rem = Remaining.
Rep = Repeat.
Rnd(s) = Round(s).
RS = Right side.
Sc = Single crochet.
Sl st = Slip stitch.
Sp(s) = Space(s).
St(s) = Stitch(es).
Tog = Together.
Tr = Treble crochet.
WS = Wrong side.

INSTRUCTIONS

The instructions are written for smaller size. If changes are necessary for larger size the instructions will be written thus ( ). Numbers for each size are shown in the same color throughout the pattern. When only one number is given in black, it applies to both sizes.

HEADBAND

Note: Ch 2 for turning ch does not count as hdc.
With MC, ch **14** (**16**) **loosely**.
1st row: (RS). 1 hdc in 3rd ch from hook. 1 hdc in each ch to end of ch. Turn. **12** (**14**) hdc.
2nd row: Ch 2. *Working in front loops only,* 1 hdc in each hdc to end of row. Turn.
Rep last row until piece from beg measures **17** (**18**) ins [**43** (**45.5**) cm], ending with a WS.
Fasten off.
Sew short ends of Headband tog.

ROSE

(See chart on page 47).
With A, ch 5. Join with sl st to form a ring.
1st rnd: Ch 3 (counts as dc). 11 dc in ring. Join with sl st to top of ch 3. 12 dc.
2nd rnd: Ch 1. *Working in front loops only,* *1 sc in next dc. *5 dc in next dc* - cluster made. Rep from * around. Join with sl st to first sc.
3rd rnd: Ch 2 (does not count as st). *Miss next sc. Keeping ch at back of work, sl st in rem back loop of next dc at base of cluster from previous rnd. Ch 3. Rep from * around. Join with sl st in same sp as first sl st.
4th rnd: Ch 1. *(1 sc. 7 dc. 1 sc) all in next ch-3 sp. Rep from * around. Join with sl st to first sc.
5th rnd: Ch 2 (does not count as working sp). *Keeping ch at back of work, sl st in rem back loop from next sc of 2nd rnd. Ch 5. Rep from * around. Join with sl st in same sp as first sl st.
6th rnd: Ch 1. *(1 sc. 3 dc. 3 tr. 3 dc. 1 sc) all in next ch-3 sp. Rep from * around. Join with sl st to first sc. Fasten off.

Sew Rose to Headband as shown in photo.

Rose

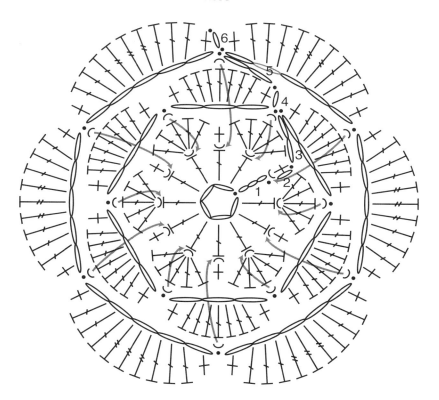

Key

◯ = chain (ch)

• = slip st (sl st)

+ = single crochet (sc)

T = double crochet (dc)

T = treble crochet (tr)

⌒ = worked in back loop only

⌣ = worked in front loop only

7b Bowtie Band

BEGINNER

SIZES

Finished circumference		
6/8	16 ins	[40.5 cm]
10/12	18 ins	[45.5 cm]

TENSION

20 sts and 26 rows = 4 ins [10 cm] in stocking st.

MATERIALS

Patons® Canadiana (100 g/3.5 oz; 187 m /205 yds)				
	Sizes	6/8	10/12	
	10022 (Oatmeal)	1	1	ball
Size 4.5 mm (U.S. 7) knitting needles **or size needed to obtain tension.**				

STITCH GLOSSARY
See page 67 for Helpful Hints.
Beg = Beginning.
K = Knit.
P = Purl.
Rep = Repeat.
RS = Right side.
St(s) = Stitch(es).
Tog = Together.

INSTRUCTIONS

The instructions are written for smaller size. If changes are necessary for larger size the instructions will be written thus ( ). Numbers for each size are shown in the same color throughout the pattern. When only one number is given in black, it applies to both sizes.

HEADBAND

Cast on **21** (**23**) sts.

1st row: (RS). K1. *P1. K1. Rep from * to end of row.

2nd row: P1. *K1. P1. Rep from * to end of row.

Rep last 2 rows until work from beg measures **15** (**15½**) ins [**38** (**39.5**) cm]. Cast off.

Sew cast on and cast off edges tog.

BOW

Cast on **17** (**19**) sts.

Work in stocking st until work from beg measures 10 ins [25.5 cm], ending with a purl row.

Cast off.

Sew cast on and cast off edges tog. Thread a running st through seam and pull tightly to gather.

BOW CENTER

Cast on 5 sts.

Work in garter st (knit every row) until work from beg measures 2 ins [5 cm]. Cast off.

FINISHING

With RS facing, wrap Bow Center around Bow over seam and sew in place. Sew Bow to Headband, concealing Headband seam.

8 Toasty Striped Set

EASY

SIZES

LEGWARMERS

To fit calf circumference		
6/8	16 ins	[40.5 cm]
10/12	18 ins	[45.5 cm]

Hat: To fit child's head size **6/8** (**10/12**).

TENSION

20 sts and 26 rows = 4 ins [10 cm] with larger needles in stocking st.

MATERIALS

Patons® Canadiana (Variegated: 100 g/3.5 oz; 175 m / 192 yds)

LEGWARMERS	Sizes	6/8	10/12	
Main Color (MC) 11712 (Happy Camper)		1	1	ball

Patons® Canadiana (Solids: 100 g/3.5 oz; 187m / 205 yds)

Contrast A 10712 (Lime Juice)		1	1	ball

Patons® Canadiana (Variegated: 100 g/3.5 oz; 175 m / 192 yds)

HAT	Sizes	6/8	10/12	
Main Color (MC) 11712 (Happy Camper)		1	1	ball

Patons® Canadiana (Solids: 100 g/3.5 oz; 187m / 205 yds)

Contrast A 10712 (Lime Juice)		1	1	ball

Sets of four sizes 4 mm (U.S. 6) and 4.5 mm (U.S. 7) double-pointed knitting needles **or size needed to obtain tension.**

STITCH GLOSSARY

See page 67 for Helpful Hints.
Approx = Approximately
Beg = Beginning.
Cont = Continue(ity).
Dec = Decrease(ing).
K = Knit.
K2tog = Knit next two stitches together.
M1 = Make 1 stitch by picking up horizontal loop lying before next stitch and knitting into back of loop.

Rep = Repeat.
P = Purl.
Pat = Pattern.
Psso = Pass slipped stitch over.
Rem = Remain(ing).
Rnd(s) = Round(s).
Sl1 = Slip next stitch knitwise.
Ssk = Slip next 2 stitches knitwise one at a time. Pass them back onto left-hand needle, then knit through back loops together.
St(s) = Stitch(es).

INSTRUCTIONS

The instructions are written for smaller size. If changes are necessary for larger size the instructions will be written thus ( ). Numbers for each size are shown in the same color throughout the pattern. When only one number is given in black, it applies to both sizes.

LEGWARMERS (make 2).

With smaller needles and A, cast on **48** (**60**) sts. Divide sts evenly on 3 needles. Join in rnd, placing marker on first st.

Work in (K2. P2) ribbing until work from beg measures 3 ins [7.5 cm].

Next rnd: *K**12** (**15**). M1. Rep from * around. **52** (**64**) sts.

Change to larger needles.
1st to 5th rnds: With MC, knit.
6th rnd: With A, knit.
7th rnd: With A, purl.
8th rnd: With A, knit.
These 8 rnds form Pat.

Cont in pat until work from beg measures approx **15** (**16**) ins [**38** (**40.5**) cm], ending with a 4th rnd.

Change to smaller needles.
Next rnd: With A, *K11(14). K2tog. Rep from * around. 48 (60) sts.
With A, work in (K2. P2) ribbing for 3 ins [7.5 cm].
Cast off in ribbing.

HAT

With smaller needles and A, cast on 88 (104) sts. Divide sts evenly on 3 needles. Join in rnd, placing marker on first st.
Work in (K2.P2) ribbing for 2 ins [5 cm].
Next rnd: *K2. M1. Rep from * around. 132 (156) sts.

Change to larger needles.
1st to 5th rnds: With MC, knit.
6th rnd: With A, knit.
7th rnd: With A, purl.
8th rnd: With A, knit.
These 8 rnds form Stripe Pat.
Rep these 8 rnds twice more.
Keeping cont of Stripe Pat, dec as follows:
Next rnd: *K7 (9). ssk. K2tog. Rep from * around. 108 (132) sts.
Work 4 rnds Stripe Pat.
Next rnd: *K5 (7). ssk. K2tog. Rep from * around. 84 (108) sts.
Work 4 rnds Stripe Pat.

Next rnd: *K3 (5). ssk. K2tog. Rep from * around. 60 (84) sts.
Work 4 rnds Stripe Pat.
Next rnd: *K1 (3). ssk. K2tog. Rep from * around. 36 (60) sts.
Work 4 rnds Stripe Pat.

Size 10/12 only: Next rnd: With MC, *K1. ssk. K2tog. Rep from * around. 48 sts.
Work 4 rnds Stripe Pat.

Both sizes: Next rnd: *Sl1. K2tog. psso. Rep from * around. 12 (16) sts.
Work 1 rnd Stripe Pat.
Next rnd: *K2tog. Rep from * around. 6 (8) sts.
Break yarn. Thread end through rem sts. Draw up tightly and fasten securely. ▲

9 Preppy Pullover

INTERMEDIATE

SIZES

To fit chest measurement			
6	25 ins	[63.5 cm	]
8	26½ ins	[67.5 cm	]
10	28 ins	[71 cm	]
12	30 ins	[76 cm	]

Finished chest			
6	30 ins	[76 cm	]
8	32 ins	[81.5 cm	]
10	34 ins	[86.5 cm	]
12	36 ins	[91.5 cm	]

TENSION

19 sts and 25 rows = 4 ins [10 cm] in stocking st with larger needles.

MATERIALS

Patons® Canadiana (100 g/3.5 oz; 187 m /205 yds)						
	Sizes	6	8	10	12	
	10022 (Oatmeal)	4	4	5	5	balls

Sizes 4 mm (U.S. 6) and 5 mm (U.S. 8) knitting needles **or size needed to obtain tension.** Cable needle. 1 stitch holder.

STITCH GLOSSARY

See page 67 for Helpful Hints.
2tog = Work next 2 stitches together.
Alt = Alternate(ing).
Beg = Beginning.
C6B = Slip next 3 stitches onto cable needle and leave at back of work. K3, then K3 from cable needle.
C6F = Slip next 3 stitches onto cable needle and leave at front of work. K3, then K3 from cable needle.
Cont = Continue(ity).
Dec = Decrease(ing).
Inc = Increase 1 stitch into next stitch by knitting into front and back of next stitch.
K = Knit.
K1tbl = Knit next stitch through back loop.
K2togtbl = Knit next 2 stitches together through back loops.
K2tog = Knit next 2 stitches together.
M1 = Make 1 stitch by picking up horizontal loop lying before next stitch and knitting into back of loop.

P = Purl.
Pat = Pattern.
P2tog = Purl next 2 stitches together.
P2togtbl = Purl next 2 stitches together through back loops.
Rem = Remaining.
Rep = Repeat.
RS = Right side.
Ssk = Slip next 2 stitches knitwise one at a time. Pass them back onto left-hand needle, then knit through back loops together.
Sl1P = Slip next stitch purlwise.
St(s) = Stitch(es).
T4B = Slip next stitch onto cable needle and leave at back of work. K3, then P1 from cable needle.
T4F = Slip next 3 stitches onto cable needle and leave at front of work. P1, then K3 from cable needle.
T5B = Slip next 2 stitches onto cable needle and leave at back of work. K3, then P2 from cable needle.
T5F = Slip next 3 stitches onto cable needle and leave at front of work. P2, then K3 from cable needle.
Tw2F = Knit into front of 2nd stitch on needle without slipping stitch off needle, then knit into front of first st and slip both stitches off needle together.
WS = Wrong side.

Knitting Needle Conversion Chart

Cdn. & U.K. Sizes	-	000	00	0	1	2	3	4	5	6	7	8	9	-	10	11	12	13	14	15
Metric Sizes (mm)	12.75	10	9	8	7.5	7	6.5	6	5.5	5	4.5	4	3.75	3.5	3.25	3	2.75	2.25	2	1.75
U.S. Sizes	17	15	13	11	-	-	10½	10	9	8	7	6	5	4	3	-	2	1	0	-

Crochet Hook Conversion Chart

Cdn. & U.K. Sizes	000	00	0	2	3	4	5	6	7	8	-	9	10	11	-	12	13	14
Metric Sizes (mm)	10	9	8	7	6.50	6	5.50	5	4.50	4	3.75	3.5	3.25	3	2.75	2.50	2.25	2
U.S. Sizes	N 15	M 13	L 11	-	K 10½	J 10	I 9	H 8	7	G 6	F 5	E 4	D 3	-	C 2	-	B 1	-

INSTRUCTIONS

The instructions are written for smallest size. If changes are necessary for larger sizes the instructions will be written thus ( ). Numbers for each size are shown in the same color throughout the pattern. When only one number is given in black, it applies to all sizes.

CABLE PANEL A (worked over 22 sts). (See Chart on page 63).
1st row: (RS). P2. K3. P3. K6. P3. K3. P2.
2nd and alt rows: Knit all knit sts and purl all purl sts as they appear.
3rd row: As 1st row.
5th row: P2. T4F. P2. K6. P2. T4B. P2.
7th row: P3. T5F. C6F. T5B. P3.
9th row: P5. (C6B) twice. P5.
11th row: P5. K3. C6F. K3. P5.
13th row: As 9th row.
15th row: P3. T5B. C6F. T5F. P3.
17th row: P2. T4B. P2. K6. P2. T4F. P2.
19th row: As 1st row.
20th row: As 2nd row.
These 20 rows form Cable Panel A.

CABLE PANEL B (worked over 6 sts). (See Chart on page 63).
1st row: (RS). K6.
2nd and alt rows: P6.
3rd and 5th rows: K6.
7th row: C6F.
8th row: Purl.
These 8 rows form Cable Panel B.

CABLE PANEL C (worked over 6 sts) (See Chart on page 63).
1st row: (RS). K6.
2nd and alt rows: P6.
3rd and 5th rows: K6.
7th row: C6B.
8th row: Purl.
These 8 rows form Cable Panel C.

BACK
****With smaller needles, cast on 74 (78-86-90) sts.
1st row: (RS). *K2. P2. Rep from * to last 2 sts. K2.
2nd row: *P2. K2. Rep from * to last 2 sts. P2.
Rep last 2 rows (K2. P2) ribbing for 2 (2½-2½-2½) ins [5 (6-6-6) cm], ending with a 2nd row and inc 12 sts evenly across last row. 86 (90-98-102) sts.

Change to larger needles and proceed in pat as follows:
1st row: (RS). (P1. K1tbl) 4 (5-7-8) times. P1. Tw2F. P2. Work 1st row Cable Panel C across next 6 sts. P2. Tw2F. (P1. K1tbl) 3 times. P1. Tw2F. Work 13th (13th-7th-1st) row Cable Panel A across next 22 sts. Tw2F. (P1. K1tbl) 3 times. P1. Tw2F. P2. Work 1st row Cable Panel B across next 6 sts. P2. Tw2F. (P1. K1tbl) 4 (5-7-8) times. P1.

2nd row: K**9** (**11**-**15**-**17**). P2. K2. Work 2nd row Cable Panel B across next 6 sts. K2. P2. K7. P2. Work **14th** (**14th**-**8th**-**2nd**) row Cable Panel A across next 22 sts. P2. K7. P2. K2. Work 2nd row Cable Panel C across next 6 sts. K2. P2. K**9** (**11**-**15**-**17**).

Last 2 rows form Shadow Rib Pat. Cable Panels A, B and C are now in position.

Cont in pat, keeping cont of Cable Panels until work from beg measures approx **11** (**11½**-**12½**-**13½**) ins [**28** (**29**-**32**-**34.5**) cm], ending with a 12th row of Cable Panel A.**

Shape armholes: Keeping cont of pat, cast off **4** (**5**-**6**-**6**) sts beg next 2 rows. **78** (**80**-**86**-**90**) sts.

Dec 1 st each end of next row and every following alt row **3** (**3**-**4**-**5**) times more. **70** (**72**-**76**-**78**) sts.

Cont even in pat until armhole measures **6** (**6½**-**7**-**7½**) ins [**15** (**16.5**-**18**-**19**) cm], ending with a WS row.

Shape shoulders: Keeping cont of pat, cast off **9** (**10**-**10**-**10**) sts beg next 2 rows, then **10** (**10**-**11**-**11**) sts beg following 2 rows. Leave rem **32** (**32**-**34**-**36**) sts on a st holder.

FRONT

Work from ** to ** as given for Back.

Shape armholes and V-neck: 1st row (RS). Keeping cont of pat, cast off **4** (**5**-**6**-**6**) sts. Pat across **35** (**36**-**39**-**41**) st (including st on needle after cast off) K2tog. K2 (neck edge). **Turn.** Leave rem st on a spare needle.

2nd row: P3. Pat to end of row.
3rd row: Work 2tog. Pat to last 4 sts. K2tog. K2 Rep last 2 rows **3** (**3**-**4**-**5**) times more. **30** (**31**-**32**-**32**) sts rem.

Next row: P3. Pat to end of row.
Next row: Pat to last 4 sts. K2tog. K2.
Rep last 2 rows **9** (**8**-**8**-**7**) times more. **20** (**22**-**23**-**24**) sts rem.

Dec 1 st at neck edge (as before) on ever following 4th row **1** (**2**-**2**-**3**) time(s) more **19** (**20**-**21**-**21**) sts rem.

Cont even in pat until armhole measure same length as Back to beg of shoulder shaping, ending with a WS row.

Shape shoulder: Cast off **9** (**10**-**10**-**10**) sts beg next row. Work 1 row even in pat. Cast off rem **10** (**10**-**11**-**11**) sts.

With RS facing, join yarn to rem sts.
1st row: K2. ssk. Pat to end of row.
2nd row: Cast off **4** (**5**-**6**-**6**) sts. Pat to last 3 sts. P3.
3rd row: K2. ssk. Pat to last 2 sts. Work 2tog.
4th row: Pat to last 3 sts. P3.
Rep last 2 rows **3** (**3**-**4**-**5**) times more. **30** (**31**-**32**-**32**) sts rem.
Next row: K2. ssk. Pat to end of row.
Next row: Pat to last 3 sts. P3.
Rep last 2 rows **9** (**8**-**8**-**7**) times more. **20** (**22**-**23**-**24**) sts rem.
Dec 1 st at neck edge (as before) on every following 4th row **1** (**2**-**2**-**3**) time(s) more. **19** (**20**-**21**-**21**) sts rem.
Cont even in pat until armhole measures same length as Back to beg of shoulder shaping, ending with a RS row.

Shape shoulder: Cast off **9** (**10**-**10**-**10**) sts beg next row. Work 1 row even in pat. Cast off rem **10** (**10**-**11**-**11**) sts.

SLEEVES

With smaller needles, cast on **42** (**46**-**46**-**50**) sts. Work **2** (**2½**-**2½**-**2½**) ins [**5** (**6**-**6**-**6**) cm] in (K2. P2) ribbing as given for Back, ending with a 2nd row and inc 6 sts evenly across last row. **48** (**52**-**52**-**56**) sts.

Change to larger needles and proceed in pat as follows:
1st row: (RS). (P1. K1tbl) **5** (**6**-**6**-**7**) times. P1. Tw2F. Work 1st row Cable Panel A across next 22 sts. Tw2F. (P1. K1tbl) **5** (**6**-**6**-**7**) times. P1.
2nd row: K**11** (**13**-**13**-**15**). P2. Work 2nd row Cable Panel A across next 22 sts. P2. K**11** (**13**-**13**-**15**).
Last 2 rows form Shadow Rib Pat. Cable Panel A is now in position.

Work a further 8 rows even in pat.
Keeping cont of pat, inc 1 st each end of next row and every following **12th** (**12th**-**10th**-**14th**) row until there are **56** (**60**-**66**-**68**) sts, taking inc sts into Shadow Rib Pat.
Cont even in pat until work from beg measures **13** (**14½**-**16**-**17**) ins [**33** (**37**-**40.5**-**43**) cm], ending with a WS row.

Shape top: Keeping cont of pat, cast off **3** (**4**-**5**-**5**) sts beg next 2 rows. **50** (**52**-**56**-**58**) sts. Dec 1 st each end of next row and every following alt row until **34** (**34**-**38**-**38**) sts rem, then on every row until 10 sts rem. Cast off in pat.

FINISHING

Pin garment pieces to measurements. Cove with a damp cloth leaving cloth to dry. Sew right shoulder seam.

V-neckband: With RS facing and smalle needles, pick up and knit **42** (**46**-**50**-**54**) st down left front neck edge. M1 at cente front (center st). Pick up and knit **42** (**46**-**50** **54**) sts up right front neck edge. K**32** (**32**-**34**-**36**) from back st holder, dec **0** (**0**-**2** **0**) sts evenly across. **117** (**125**-**133**-**145**) sts
1st row: (WS). *P2. K2. Rep from * to cente 5 sts. P2. K1. P2. **K2. P2. Rep from ** to end of row.
2nd row: *K2. P2. Rep from * to center 5 sts K2tog. P1. K2togtbl. **P2. K2. Rep from * to end of row.
3rd row: Rib to center 5 sts. P2togtbl. K1 P2tog. Rib to end of row.
4th row: Rib to center 5 sts. K2tog. P1 K2togtbl. Rib to end of row.
5th row: As 3rd row.
Cast off in ribbing, dec as before. Sew lef shoulder and neckband seam.

Sew in sleeves. Sew side and sleeve seams

Cable Panel A

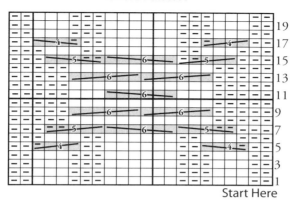

Start Here

Cable Panel B

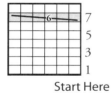

Start Here

Cable Panel C

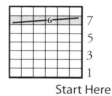

Start Here

Key

☐ = Purl on RS rows. Knit on WS rows.
☐ = Knit on RS rows. Purl on WS rows.
= C6B
= C6F
= T4B
= T4F
= T5B
= T5F

Preppy Pullover   63

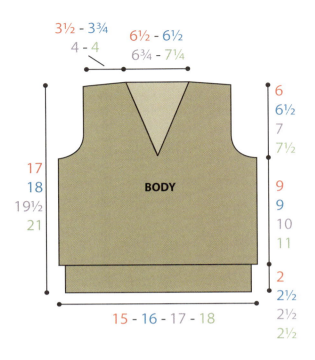
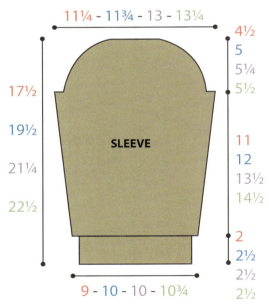

Learn to Knit Instructions

Casting On

1. Loop the yarn as shown and slip needle under the lower strand of the loop.
2. Tighten the slip knot, leaving the other end approx 4 ins [10 cm] long.

3a, b. Insert the right-hand needle through slip knot and wind yarn over right-hand needle. Pull loop through slip knot.

4. Place new loop on left-hand needle beside first loop [2 stitches (sts) on left-hand needle].

5. Insert right-hand needle between sts on left-hand needle and wind yarn over right-hand needle.

6. Pull loop through. Place this new loop on left-hand needle beside last st. Repeat (rep) steps 5 and 6 until required number of sts have been cast on.

The Knit Stitch

1. Hold the needle with cast on sts in your left hand with yarn at the back of work. Insert right-hand needle from left to right through the front of the first st on the left-hand needle.

2. Wind yarn over right-hand needle.

3. Draw yarn through this original st which forms a new st.

4. Slip the original st off left-hand needle, keeping new st on right-hand needle.

5. Rep steps 1 to 4 until all sts have been transferred to right-hand needle. Transfer needle with sts to your left hand to knit the next row.

The Purl Stitch

1. With yarn at front of work, insert right-hand needle from right to left through front of first st on left-hand needle.

2. Wind yarn over right-hand needle. Pull yarn through st.

3. Slip original st off needle. Rep these steps until all sts have been transferred onto right-hand needle.

Increasing and Decreasing

Increase 1 st in next st by working into front and back of st as follows: Knit st then, before slipping it off needle, twist right-hand needle behind left-hand needle and knit again into back of loop. Slip original st off needle. There are now 2 sts made from original stitch.

K2tog Decrease Knit 2 sts together (tog) through the front of both loops.

P2tog Decrease Purl 2 sts tog through the front of both loops.

Casting Off

Cast off using knit stitch (knitwise) Knit the first 2 sts. *Using left-hand needle, lift 1st st over 2nd st and drop it off needle. Knit the next st; rep from * until all sts have been worked and only 1 st remains on the right-hand needle. Cut yarn (leaving enough to sew in end) and thread cut end through st on needle. Draw yarn up firmly to fasten off last st.

Cast off using purl stitch (purlwise) Purl first 2 sts. *Using left-hand needle, lift 1st st over 2nd st and drop it off needle. Purl next st; rep from * securing the last st as described above.

Learn to Crochet Instructions

Slip Knot

Make a loop, then hook another loop through it.

Tighten gently and slide the knot up to the hook.

Slip Stitch (sl st)

Insert hook into work (second chain from hook), yarn over hook (yoh) and draw the yarn through both the work and loop on hook in one movement.

To join a chain ring with a slip stitch (sl st), insert hook into first chain (ch), yarn over hook (yoh) and draw through both the work and the yarn on hook in one movement.

Half Double Crochet (hdc)

1. Yarn over hook (yoh) and insert the hook into the work [3rd chain (ch) from hook on starting chain].

2. Yarn over hook (yoh) and draw through the work only.

3. Yarn over hook (yoh) again and draw through all three loops on the hook.

4. 1 hdc made. Yarn over hook (yoh), insert hook into next stitch (st); repeat (rep) from step 2.

Chain Stitch (ch)

Yarn over hook (yoh) and draw the yarn through to form a new loop without tightening up the previous one.

Repeat to form as many chains (ch) as required. Do not count the slip knot as a stitch.

Single Crochet (sc)

1. Insert the hook into the work [2nd chain (ch) from hook on starting chain], *yarn over hook (yoh) and draw yarn through the work only.

2. Yarn over hook (yoh) again and draw the yarn through both loops on the hook.

3. 1 single crochet made. Insert hook into next stitch: repeat (rep) from * in step 1.

Double Crochet (dc)

1. Yarn over hook (yoh), insert hook into work (4th chain from hook on starting chain).

2. Yarn over hook (yoh), draw through the work only.

3. Yarn over hook (yoh), draw through first two loops only.

4. Yarn over hook (yoh) draw through last two loops on hook.

5. 1 dc made. Yarn over hook (yoh), insert hook into next stitch, repeat from step 2.